arabic, between love and war

FIRST EDITION

trace: translating [x] series
Editors, *Arabic, between Love and War*: Yasmine Haj and Norah Alkharashi
Cover and Book Design: Prerana Das
Series Editor: Nuzhat Abbas

Arabic, between Love and War
ISBN 978-1-7752567-6-2 [softcover]
ISBN 978-1-7752567-7-9 [e-book]

Cataloguing in Publication available from Library and Archives Canada

*We ask our writers, translators, artists, and readers to question borders and unsettle various
forms of local and global colonialism and coloniality. We are grateful to do our work in
Tkaronto in solidarity with diverse indigenous peoples from across Turtle Island who continue
to gather upon the traditional lands of many nations including the Mississaugas of the Credit,
the Anishnabeg, the Chippewa, the Haudenosaunee and the Wendat. This territory was the
subject of the Dish With One Spoon Wampum Belt Covenant, an agreement between the Iroquois
Confederacy and Confederacy of the Ojibwe and allied nations to peaceably share and care for the
resources around the Great Lakes.*

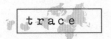

tracepress.org

Printed and bound in Canada

arabic, between love and war

edited by Yasmine Haj and Norah Alkharashi

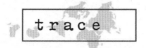

trace: translating [x] is a process based publication series emerging from trace's occasional series of creative workshops and community-centred collaborations. Each text in the series engages, in different ways, with the challenges of writing and literary translation, exploring the ways in which decolonial, antiracist, feminist, and queer practices can help unsettle literary archives and the present.

Facilitated by Yasmine Haj and Norah Alkharashi, trace: translating [x] Arabic workshops (2022-2023) invited translators living and working with/in Arabic to explore processes of loss and unlearning encountered on their path to translation as critical creation.

Our gratitude to all the workshop participants who entered our virtual space and enlivened it with passionate thought, conversation, and creative labour. Although not all participants developed work for publication, their presence and questions have helped guide the development of the project and this collection.

Series Editor: Nuzhat Abbas

table of contents

تنهيدة
intervals

حرب
war

To Speak to Each Other

Yasmine Haj

~

1947. Cutting trees and life short has yet to be fused into inhabitants that feel but fail to imagine.

Palestine is not biblical; it is exquisite, and unexceptional. It has seashores, herbs, springs, valleys, songs, textiles, and people, just like any other land. To be coveted, however, time and again, will turn anything biblical.

1947, and the phoenix is yet to be formed.

Palestine doesn't know it will become the nemesis and love of the world, or that its Nakba will reverberate through Iraq, Lebanon, Libya, Sudan, Syria, and Yemen, pulsing southwards, eastwards, to connect our struggles, loves, and wars against a grand list of oppressive systems.

Palestine doesn't yet know that other sites of catastrophe—courtesy of Sikes, Picot, Balfour, and multiple axes of cobalt, blood diamonds, gas, petrol, and blood money—will become visibilized along its histories of resistance and continuity, gathering force and drawing innumerable captives of imperialism into one place and time continuum.

*

2023, and we learn to say *no*.

We watch the European-made clock tick, and we deconstruct the numbers as we sing to summon the collective spirit of 2025 or 2026, depending on the astrological counter we use, depending on the prophecy we receive. We count the minutes as a musician on his yellow motorbike asks us to pray for peace, but we pray for liberation.

How do we pray for something that never was? Do we translate justice, and by doing so, create it with our empty manmade words that keep oiling the genocidal machines? Do words suffice when what has been cut is wordless? When nothing is left to lose, poetry can barely matter—a venomous cycle of words.

*

2024. Palestine remains, a blessing and a curse—waiting to be liberated in order to liberate—just as its past and future counterparts, lands of an alleged postcolonial world, await their liberation to liberate it.

Here come the keffiyehs, everywhere, speaking volumes. Graffiti everywhere: *down with the colonisers.* Everywhere symbols: the four colours of blood, earth, purity of heart, and confrontation. And here goes Palestine, continuing up the path ahead, in tears but with words as well. Here it goes, centring and decentring itself alongside partners in struggle, revealing a mistranslation, a separation, imposed for far too long.

Here goes Palestine, having learned English for more than a hundred years, because it had to—to speak back, to sing, and to translate itself as it wishes, for the most part—just as its predecessors in struggle set up the path, ages ago, translating themselves into German, French, Italian, Portuguese, and Spanish.

But what if our words, our bodies, our lives, had never needed translation?

The act of translation is, perhaps, as much a summons to perform in front of those who have othered us, as it is an invitation to impart knowledge. Pedagogy and performance go hand in hand because geopolitics demands it. But what if we imagined a different paradigm and began to create and rise within it? What if we translated to learn from, and to speak to each other, rather than perform to the panopticon?

*

2024, and Palestine has finally humanized itself enough before the skeptical to complement the resilience and resistance of its people and their contiguous allies. Palestine cries and tries to re-rise from the ashes, along with Congo, Iraq, Kanaky, Lebanon, Sudan, Syria, Yemen, and many, many more. There are far too many.

Palestine is finally speaking out loud enough—with words, with shrieks, with howls—with the oppressed around the world, inviting them to join forces, inviting them to re-read their past, to unlearn it, to rewrite it ...

No, writing is too docile. The future must be carved out.

*

May the poems gathered here, in translation and in their original voice, spark introspection, remedy, and acts of imagination in between. May they inspire love—to share, to carry on, to resist—each to their own compass, regulated in community.

May they also remind us that no words can pave sense into our wounds. May those entities that have burned our peoples alive be dismantled, everywhere. May poetry heal all that is left of our souls to help us rage on.

Between Impossibility and Necessity

Norah Alkharashi

❧

The art of literary translation is often said to be both impossible and necessary. Impossible because no linguistic code is commensurable with any other—particularly so in the case of poetic language which, being among the most refined and expressive of literary forms, is expected to have myriad and complex nuances. Yet translation remains necessary. Without it, there would be no conversation across linguistic and cultural barriers, no prospect of the mutual understanding that remains a prerequisite for the peaceful, emancipated life towards which we are all striving.

What has guided this work, from our workshops for `trace: translating [x] Arabic` and our public readings, through the process of creating this book, is a conviction that creative translation is indispensable to our common, shared experience of being human. At the same time, we invited translators to consider questions of history, power, and privilege, and how these affect the ways in which translation moves through the world. The poems gathered in this collection have been selected by each translator based on their own interests and poetic affinities. Here, we find words that move fluidly between themes of love and war; between differences of region, time, gender, age, race, ethnicity, and class; and between Arabic and English; offering insights, both poetic and political, that resonate beyond the original tongue.

From the start of our editing process, we wanted to intensify the translators' choices, honouring each distinct decision, but also honouring the fidelity of each translator to the voice of the original author. Located within, or moving between various regions and registers of the Arabic-speaking world and its diasporas, these translators skilfully explore the tension between shaping poems for varied audiences while remaining faithful to the culturally specific contexts they were written in. The vibrant literary discussions in Arabic that took place during workshops, and the familiarity forged during the editorial process, allowed us to better understand each text from the translator's vantage. We became more confident as we edited, and worked closely with the translators to refine the texts as needed, with each translation answering back to the source text, sensitive to the original, even as it stood up as a work in its own right.

These poems encourage the reader into conversation not only with the poets and their translators, but also the worlds made manifest through their voices and words.

love

Whether in Arabic, English, or otherwise, the noun of love is often complemented with a falling verb. Falling into, and rising out of love plunges us into new constructs—language announces them into being.

للحُبِّ أُغني
لميعة عباس عمارة

لكَ أنتَ أُغني
حبُّكَ أنتَ هو الخالد
أعداءُ الأمسِ على جُثثِ القتلى
تشربُ من نَخْبٍ واحد.

لكَ أنتَ أُغنّي
صوتُكَ يختصرُ التاريخَ إلى أغوارِ الصمتِ
تُشبِهُكَ الدنيا – تختصرُ الكونَ –
وأنتَ ... خُلاصتُها أنت.

للبحرِ شبيهِكَ أكتبُ شِعري
أَتَنَشَّقُ مِلءَ الرئتينِ على الشاطئ
سفنًا لم يدهَمْها القرصانُ
وحورياتٍ
ولآلئٍ
لسماءِ اللهِ أُغنّي
زرقةُ هذا السقفِ المتناهي البُعدْ
وحبُّكَ
شيئانِ بلا حَدْ،
فليتوزَّعْ مجدُ الشعرِ على الشعراء
حينَ تمرُّ فصولُ العام
تَتَبَدَّلُ ألوانُ الأشجارِ وأوزانُ الأشعارِ
وأحوالُ الرؤساء.
ويظلُّ الحُبُّ هو الخالد
إذ أعداءُ الأمسِ على جُثثِ القتلى
تشربُ من نَخْبٍ واحد.

For Love I Sing

Lamia Abbas Amara

Translated from Arabic by Hiba Moustafa

For you I sing.
Only your love is eternal
while yesterday's enemies, over dead bodies,
share a toast.

For you I sing.
Your voice condenses history to the depths of silence
the world resembles you—the universe is contained in it—
and you ... you are its essence.

To the sea, your image, I write my poems.
On the beach, I take a lungful
of ships not plundered by pirates
of mermaids,
of pearls.
To the sky of God, I sing.
This distant blue dome
and your love
two infinite things.
Let the glory of poetry be shared among poets.
As seasons change
the colours of trees change
the meter of verses change
and tyrants* change their colours.
Only love is eternal
while yesterday's enemies, over dead bodies,
share a toast.

---

* I took the liberty of using the word 'tyrants' when it should have been 'presidents' to match
the original. Is it really just 'presidents' who share a toast over our dead bodies, or also kings,
emirs, princes, and prince regents? The list is too long. And 'tyrants' seemed more comprehen-
sive and truer to reality. The region is full of them.

قصائد حب
سمر دياب

أحبّ أن أناديك: يا حبيبي
لأني أشعر حينها بأنهم لم يدمّروا مدننا
وأن الأشجار التي احترقت في الجبال ليست حقيقية
يا حبيبي ...
لم تحدث حرب
لم يحدث شيء ...

*

أريد أن أحبك من دون حرب
لكن من دون ورود أيضًا
لأن الورود تتشاجر حين لا تجد شيئًا تفعله
وتنتحر حين ننظر إليها كثيرًا
لا أريد حربًا
لا أريد ورودًا
لا أريد شيئًا أبدًا
سوى ألّا يخلو العالم من الجُزر الصغيرة
هناك حيث يمكن أن نبكي
لأن السماء نقصت بعض النجوم
وإلى الأبد
يرنّ البحر في الهواء

*

أحبّ الغابة أكثر من البحر
وأتمنى أن تقبّلني هناك
حيث لا أسماك بعيون مفتوحة إلى الأبد حولنا
ولا قاع نرتطم به سوى أشجار طويلة
ولا ماء سوى في بئرٍ لا يعرفها سوانا
ولا ملح سوى في صهيل الأحصنة البرية البعيدة

*

24

Love Poems

Samar Diab

Translated from Arabic by Nofel

I love calling you *habibi*
because then I feel as though they haven't destroyed our cities
and that the trees burning in the mountains are not real.
O habibi ...
the war didn't happen
nothing happened ...

*

I want to love you without war
but without flowers either
because flowers fight when they have nothing to do
because flowers die by suicide when stared at for too long.
I don't want war.
I don't want flowers.
I want nothing at all
but for the world not to be emptied of small islands.
There, where we can weep
because the sky lost a few stars
and the sea rings forever in the air.

*

I love the forest more than the sea
and I wish you would kiss me there
where no open-eyed fish are perpetually around us
no seabed to bump against, only long trees
no water besides that of a well only we know of
no salt other than in the whickering of faraway wild horses.

*

كلما أغمضت عيني
تهجم عليّ الأشجار
أفتحهما تختفي
حبيبي يظنني نائمة ...
وأنا أتجوّل في الغابة

Whenever I close my eyes
trees attack me.
I open my eyes,
they disappear.
Habibi thinks I'm asleep ...
but I'm roaming the forest.

كلمة واحدة تكفي
علي محمود خضير

عامٌ
ينعَسُ
على مهلٍ

على شجرةٍ
جُرحٌ بين حمامةٍ وغُصن
ومائدةٍ لشخصٍ
لم يأتِ.

تذكّرتُكِ
تذكّرتُ الصمتَ يَخضلُ
والشجرةَ التي ظَللتنا
والعطرَ يدنو.

لم أعرفْ
أننا على الحافّةِ من كلِّ شيءٍ
وأنَّ كلمةً واحدة
تكفي لتيبسَ الشجرة
ويصيرَ الصمتُ ظِلًا
والقلبُ خزانة أُمّ.

لا ظِلَّ في روحي الآن
فقد سَقطتُ
بكلمةٍ واحدةٍ سقطتُ
كأنّي حائطٌ
من زجاج.

One Word

Ali Mahmoud Khudayyir
Translated from Arabic by Zeena Faulk

This year
    is dozing off
    slowly.

On a tree
a wound lies between a dove and a branch.
and a table for one
    who never showed up.

I remembered you!
    I remembered the silence growing slightly wet,
    and the tree that shaded us,
    and the fragrance drawing near.

    I didn't know
that we were on the edge of everything
and that one word
alone was enough to wither a tree,
    that silence turns into shade,
    and the heart a safe haven for pain.

    No shadow remains in my soul now,
    for I have fallen,
with one word I fell,
as if I were a glass
    wall.

اليمامة الأسيرة
إيمان أبو خضرا
ترجمتهُ عن الإنكليزيّة إيمان أبو خضرا

هل تراني؟
أنا هنا يا حبيبي
جئتَنا رجلًا على يد الظلام ترعرع
قلبُك المكسور تَعِبَ من الحياة
إلى لحظة عدالة يتطلّع

لكن في نظري حبيبي
لازلت ذاك الطفل الذي لم أحضنه مُودِّعةً
تلك اليمامة ذات الثلاثة عشرَ عامًا
بريئةً وجامحةً
بجناحيها للتحليق مُتشوّقة

وسطَ ضجيج الحضور
أسمع سكونَك
تلتقي عينانا، يتوقّف الزمن
من تحت الكَمامة ألمحُ اعتلالَك
وسبع سنواتٍ طِوال عليك موشومة

أنا هنا يا حبيبي
انظر إليّ، بجانبك أقف
كشجرة زيتون شامخة
يقتلعونني لكن إلى جانبك أظل
بقوّةٍ عن بُعد بِكَ مُتَمسِّكة

Captive Dove

Eman Abukhadra

Do you see me?
I am here, my love.
You walk in, a man
raised by darkness,
your broken heart, tired of life,
longing for a moment of justice.

For me, habibi,
you are still the child
I never hugged goodbye.
My thirteen-year-old dove,
innocent and wild,
with wings eager to fly.

In the tumultuous crowd
I hear your stillness.
Our eyes meet, time stops.
Beneath that mask
I catch a glimpse of your illness,
and the seven long years, tattooed across.

I am here, my love.
Look at me, I stand by you
like a towering olive tree.
They pull me away
but I remain beside you,
holding you close, from afar.

اسمع قلبي ينبضُ في صدرك
راقب رئتي تتنفسان عطرك
حُس بأناملي تُقبل ندوب رسغك
وكن على ثقة، قصارى جهدي سأبذل
فملاكُك الحارس أنا،
وأنت رغم الظلام نجمي الساطع

يداي مُكبّلتان تمامًا كيديك
معًا نُشاهِدنا نذبل
بُنَيّ لا تستسلم
سنُحطِّم هذه الأبواب
والعدالة ستسود يومًا

أعلم أنّهم كسروا روحك
وأطفأوا شعلة عينيك الخلابتين
جسدُك المُعذّب مُخدّر الآن، ولكن
رأسك لا تكبت الصرخات
ما عُدتَ تذكر الحقيقة
لكنّنا أكاذيبهم نتتبع

من بين ضلوعي اقتُلع قلبي، ينوح
وهم يجرّونك يا صغيري إلى الهاوية
كتفيكَ المتعبتين قد نامتا
قدميك الغاضبتين تدوسان قبلة الأمل

سأُرفرف حولك روحًا يائسة
لأُفزع الظلام
فليطمئنّ بالُك صغيري، ويالله تنام يالله تنام
لأجلك سأحارب ولن أتوقف أبدًا
حتى يرجع عصفوري الصغير إلى عشّه

Listen to my heart pound in your chest,
watch my lungs breathe in your scent,
feel my fingers kiss your scarred wrist,
and trust, I will do my absolute best.
I am your guardian angel, and you,
despite the darkness, my shining star.

My hands are tied
just like yours.
We watch ourselves wither away
but don't surrender, my son.
We will smash these doors
and justice will prevail, one day.

I know, they broke your spirit,
extinguished the fire in your beautiful eyes.
Your tortured body has grown numb
but your head can't hold back the cries.
You no longer remember the truth,
but we are keeping track of their lies.

Ripped out of my chest, my heart weeps
as they drag you, my child, into the abyss.
Your shoulders, tired, are asleep
as your angry feet trample on hope's kiss.

Like a desperate soul, I'll hover around you
and scare the darkness away.
Hush my baby, let your mind rest.
I will fight for you. I will not stop,
until my little bird is back in his nest.

---

* Ahmad Manasra was arrested in 2015, when he was thirteen. He remains imprisoned, despite being found innocent, and suffers from poor mental health after prolonged solitary confinement. I wrote this poem in 2023, after witnessing his mother's anguish.

العصفور
قاسم سعودي

هل تعرفين لماذا لم يخلقني الله عصفورًا؟
كان يعلم أنَّكِ جناحي المكسور
لذلك
أنا أنزِف الآن في الأعالي
وأسقط
مثل طفلٍ يتيمٍ لم يتعلّم المشي

The Sparrow

Qasim Saudi

Translated from Arabic by Ibrahim Fawzy

Do you know why God did not create me a sparrow?
He knew you would be my broken wing.
So now
I bleed in the heights
fall
like an orphaned child who never learned to walk.

قبلة

سمر دياب

كان الجميع خائفًا
الرجال والنساء والأطفال
وددتُ لو أنهض من سريري وأخبرهم أنّ كلّ شيء على ما يرام
هذه عروقٌ نافرة في السماء
تظهر حين يقبّلني
لكنّي غفوت ثانيةً
وحين استيقظت
لم أجد أحدًا، لم أجد شيئًا
سوى سماء تنبض فوق مدن مهجورة
عودوا ...
إنّها قبلة
إنّها قبلة

Kiss

Samar Diab

Translated from Arabic by Nofel

Everyone was afraid
men and women and children.
I wanted to get off my bed and tell them that everything was fine
these were veins throbbing in the sky
they show up when he kisses me
but I fell asleep again
and when I woke up
I found no one, I found nothing
except for a sky beating over abandoned cities
Come back ...
It's a kiss
It's a kiss

فجّري هذه الشرايين

دعد حدّاد

اكتبي، اكتبي، اكتبي
فجّري هذه الشرايين
اسفحي فوق الألواح الخشبية المتآكلة
حتى يخرج دود الأرض
من كل الشقوق
اقفزي فوق السياجات
احملي هذه الأتربة ... من فوق صدري
لا ... تهدهديني

٣١ كانون الأول ١٩٨٥

Explode These Veins

Daad Haddad

Translated from Arabic by Rana Issa and Suneela Mubayi

Write, write, write
explode these veins
spill like blood over these eroded wooden planks
until the earthworms come out
from all the cracks
jump over the fences
lift this soil ... off my chest.
Do not ... cradle me.

December 31, 1985

وقطر السّماء
دعد حدّاد

يبكي الله لأنّي أحبّك أكثر منه
وتمطر السماءُ حين أفتّش عنك
وأخاف، فأبكي ...
وأؤجّل لقائي معك

صباح ٩ نيسان ١٩٨٦

And the Sky Rains

Daad Haddad

Translated from Arabic by Rana Issa and Suneela Mubayi

God weeps because I love you more than him.
The sky rains when I search for you
and I am frightened, so I weep ...
and delay seeing you.

Morning, April 9, 1986

يا أغاني الماضي
دعد حدّاد

ماذا توشوش لها في الأماسي
وهي تبكي؟
تجاعيدها القلبية
تغني على زندها وحدها
وتراسل الطيور
يتأتّى في حضنها الرجال
ويُسلَّم مفتاحُها
ويُغلق بابُ كونها
وتولدُ في الشهر
مرتين
يا أغاني الماضي!
يا أغاني عقلة الأصبع
يا أغاني الدور البعيدة
يا أغاني الليل
دود الصّيف "قُومْ صلّي"
وتولدُ دعد
على مقعد ... في حديقة
وتستقبل أعوامَها
وتبكي على الراحلين
وتفرح أنّ القصيدة عادت إلى حزنها
وتبكي على حضنها
وتبكي على مقعد في الحديقة

فجر ٣١ آذار ١٩٨٦

To the Songs of the Past

Daad Haddad

Translated from Arabic by Rana Issa and Suneela Mubayi

What do they whisper to her in the evening as she weeps?
Her heart's wrinkles
sing alone on her forearm
and send messages to the birds.
Men manifest themselves in her lap
her key is handed over
the door to her universe is shut
and she is born twice
in a month.
O songs of the past!
The songs of Little Thumbling
The songs of faraway abodes
The songs of the night
Get up and pray,
summer worms*
and Daad is born
on a bench ... in a park.
She welcomes her years
and mourns the departed.
She is overjoyed that the poem has returned to its sorrow.
She weeps in her own lap
and weeps on a bench ... in the park.

Dawn, March 31, 1986

---

* A colloquial expression alluding to the coming of summer, when certain kinds
of worms emerge from the soil.

أنا أحب إفريقيا

قاسم سعودي

أنا أحب إفريقيا
أحب أن أصعد على الفيل الأحمر
أشارك الناس هناك حروبهم الطويلة
أعد الطعام للمحاربين
فأنا لا أقوى على حمل السهام
أو الرماح الثقيلة
لكن هنا
ومن أعلى المنزل
وقبل اللحظة التي تهمسين بها أحبك
كانت تطوقنا المدرعات كل ليلة
وتمتد الفوهات
لا لشيء
فقط لأني صرخت أيضًا أحبك
أنا الآن على سطح الغرفة
(الغرفة التي شيّدتها أمي لزواج أخي الصغير لكنه لم يكمل الحياة)
أقيس المسافة من بغداد إلى إفريقيا
وعلى ظهري رمح طويل
وعشر بنادق سريعة
وأخت صغيرة تبكي وتقول :
متى تعود إلى رأسك يا أخي؟

44

I love Africa

Qasim Saudi

Translated from Arabic by Ibrahim Fawzy

I love Africa.
I'd love to ride a red elephant
to join the people in their long wars.
I'd prepare the warriors' food;
I'm not strong enough to bear arrows
or heavy spears.
But here, in this place
from the top of the house,
right before you professed your love,
armoured vehicles encircled us at night
their barrels drawn out
for no reason
other than crying out, *I love you, too.*
I am now above my brother's room
(a room my mother built for my younger brother's wedding,
his life cut short.)
I measure the distance from Baghdad to Africa's shore
as a long spear rests on my back
with ten swift rifles.
A little sister weeps:
When will you come back to your senses, brother?

تنهيدة

intervals

Here are acts of love, loss, and mourning, and the political act of surrendering to hope. These are liminal spaces where wars of flesh and love—ongoing, past, or yet to pass—have lingered, holding hearts and words in limbo, with beats yet to be translated.

درب الدموع

(إلى السكان الأصليين الذي اقتُلعوا من أرضهم وشُتِّتوا في المنافي القاحلة)
ميلاد فايزة

لم أقتل أحدًا
ولكنهم يطرقون كلَّ ليلةٍ بابَ بيتي
ويتركونَ لي رسائل غامضة
محفورةً على الجدران بالخناجر والأظافر
يعودون حاملين رفات قتلاهم في سلالٍ من القصب
ودماؤهم تقطر على العشبِ
وأوراقِ شجر القَيْقبِ

لم أقتل أحدًا أقول لهم
ولكنهم يأتون ليلًا
متخفّين
لامرئيّينَ
يجلسون أمامي
ويقرؤون عليّ لائحة الاتهام بلغةٍ تصفّر في ثناياها الريحُ

لم أقتل أحدًا أقول لهم
ولكنهم يهزّون أكتافهم لامبالينَ بحيرتي
يشيرون إلى أشجار الخوخِ والتفاح في حديقتي
ويملؤونَ البيت صخبًا

لستُ من وضع السُمّ لكم في النهر
أو علّق في أعناق آلهتكم نجمات ذابلة
أريهم أوْشامًا أمازيغية على كتفي
وحقولًا كانَ يحرثُها أبي بأصابع يديه المتعرّقتيْنِ
وترجماتٍ لم تنتهِ لشاعرٍ فقد ذراعه في حربٍ منسية
لكنهم يهزّون أكتافهم
ويسدلونَ على النوافذ الستائرَ
ويرقصون على إيقاع طبولٍ يأتي من بعيد

48

Trail of Tears

(To indigenous peoples, uprooted from their lands, and dispersed in arid exiles)
Miled Faiza
Translated from Arabic by Miled Faiza and Karen McNeil

I didn't kill anyone
yet they knock on the door of my house every night.
They leave mysterious messages
carved on the walls with daggers and nails.
They come back carrying the corpses of their dead in bamboo
baskets, their blood dripping on grass
and the maple leaves.

I didn't kill anyone, I say to them.
Yet they come at night
disguised,
invisible.
They sit in front of me
reading the list of accusations in a language with wind whistling
through its layers.

I didn't kill anyone, I say to them,
but they shrug, indifferent to my confusion.
They point to the peach and apple trees in my yard, and fill the
house with noise.

It wasn't me who poisoned your river
and hung pale stars from the necks of your gods.
I show them Amazighi tattoos on my shoulders,
and the fields that my father ploughed with the sweat of his hands,
and unfinished translations of a poet who lost his arm in a
forgotten war, but they just shrug.
They pull down the window shades
and dance to the sound of a faraway drum.

أقف في ظلمة البيت وأرقص معهم
أدخلُ دائرةً من البخور
حاملًا على رأسي قرابيني
وحين يغادرون البيت فجرًا
لا يقولون شيئًا
يتسلّقونَ خيوط الضوء واحدًا إثر واحد
أقسمُ لهم إني لم أقتل أحدًا
ثم آخذُ أطفالي
والغريبة التي أينعت بذورُها في دمي
وأمشي مع النهر
أمشي وراءهم عابرًا غاباتٍ أحرقها الغزاةُ

أهذهِ طريق البيت؟ تسألني بنتي ذات الأعوام الخمسة
وتسقط لعبةٌ خشبية من يدها
تسقط نجمةٌ كانت قبلتنا
بيتنا أرضُ الله الواسعة أقول لها
خيمةٌ في الصحراء
أو كوخٌ تحت سنديانة معمّرة
نمشي في دربِ الدموع
في قافلة من المنفيين خلف حُلمٍ لا يتّسع للغزاة
وصباحٍ لا تجرحهُ رصاصةٌ عابرة

I stand up in the dark of the house and dance with them.
I enter a circle of incense,
carrying my offerings on my head.
And when they leave at dawn
they don't say anything.
They climb the threads of light, one after another.
I swear to them that I didn't kill anyone.
Then I carry my children,
and the stranger whose seeds sprouted in my blood,
and walk along the river.
I walk behind them across forests burned by the invaders.

Is this the way home? My five-year-old daughter asks me,
a wooden toy falls from her hand,
a star that used to be our qiblah.
Our house is God's wide earth, I say to her,
a tent in the desert,
or the shade under an old oak tree.
We would walk in the trail of tears
in a caravan of the exiled,
behind a dream that doesn't have room for invaders,
and a morning not scratched by stray bullets.

أقدامٌ لا تستطيع الوصول

نور بعلوشة

أريد عينين باستطاعتهما البكاء طيلة الوقت
وأقدامًا بإمكانها الوصول لشيءٍ لا أعرفه
فهناك شيءٌ لا نعرفه زيد أن نعود إليه
مثلما تعود البراري لطبيعتها
فتصرخ
مثلما تعود الابتسامات لطبيعتها
فتتخفّى
مثلما تعود الشوارع لطبيعتها
فتتذكّر أقدام العابرين

أريد شيئًا أعود إليه
وبابًا خلفيًّا للهرب
أريد عناقًا مع كلّ الأشياء الّتي فقدتُها دفعةً واحدة
وعليه فإنّني أريد بئرًا من الأيادي والأجساد
أريد عودًا أستند عليه
وطريقًا أمشي إليه
ودمعةً أضع فيها كلّ المرافئ الدافئة والحكايات
علّها تذوب
علّ الملح الذائب فيها
يصبح شيئًا جديدًا
حتّى لو أصبح دميةً
سأحبّها

أريد شاطئًا
أحبّه ويحبّني
ويحبّنا
أريد ضوءًا
لا يشعّ
ولا يدخل في مكان

Feet Unable to Arrive

Nour Balousha

Translated from Arabic by Nashwa Nasreldin

I want two eyes that can withstand all the weeping
and feet that can arrive at something I don't know
because there is a thing we don't know; it is there we wish to return
like the prairie that returns to its natural state
and shrieks
like the smiles that return to their natural state
and hide
like the roads that return to their natural state
and ruminate over the footsteps of passersby

I want something to return to
and a backdoor to escape
I want to embrace everything I lost in one fell swoop
I want a well crammed with hands and limbs
I want a rod to lean on
and a road to walk on
and a tear I can drop into all the warm harbours and stories
so it may dissolve
so the salt dissolved within it
can mutate into something new
even if it morphs into a doll
I'll hold it dear

I want a beach
to love and which will love me
and love us
I want a light
that does not radiate
nor enters any place

أريده حقيقيًّا
أريده أن يبني
أن يعيد شيئًا
أن يتّجه نحونا

أريد أن يعود طفلٌ واحدٌ للحياة
ولو جاء مغبَّشًا
وباكيًا
أريده أن يأتي
أريد أن أركض
نحو شيءٍ ما
ليس غابةً
ليس بحرًا
ليس قصّةً
إنّما فكرةٌ
فكرةٌ واحدةٌ عن الأمان
اختفتْ في بئرٍ من الموتى
واليتامى

I want it to be real
I want it to build
to restore something
to move towards us

I want one child to come back to life
even if he came back blurred
and weeping
I want him to come
I want to run
towards something
not a forest
not an ocean
not a story
but an idea
a single idea about safety
that disappeared in a well of corpses
and orphans

الشعراء الصامتون

دعد حدّاد

كيف يخرّبون العالم
هؤلاء الشعراء الصامتون!
كيف يهجّون الغيرةَ
ويصمدون كآلهة
كيف يتداولون...فتات الخبز!
آه، كيف يكون من كثرة الحبّ!
آه هذه الزوايا العينية
هذه الحلاوات
هذه الضحكات
خذ هذه السوسنة
خذ هذا الشراب المُسكر
وخذ حرّيّة

ليل ٢٣ شباط ١٩٨٦

The Silent Poets

Daad Haddad

Translated from Arabic by Rana Issa and Suneela Mubayi

How they destroy the world
those silent poets!
how they articulate jealousy,
how they stand unmoved, godlike,
how they exchange ... bread crumbs!
Oh, how they cry from too much love!
Oh, their sideways glances,
their saccharine pleasures,
their laughs.
Pick this lily,
drink this intoxicant,
and with it,
take some freedom.

Nighttime, February 23rd, 1986

المعهد

نجلاء عثمان التوم

يمكن السير في متاهة مكوّنة من كلمة واحدة،
لخمسين عام،
أو جمع الحطب من شخير الغابة،
إشعال نارٍ صغيرة ترجِع القابلة المدخّنة؛
اسمها نجاة.

نجاة، نجاة
نشأت مع أجواز البط المنزلي المتسخ دائمًا،
وتعلّمت التوليد في معهد.

المعهد
المعهد
المتاهة المكوّنة من امرأة واحدة
تتدحرج، مثل قنفذ شوكي،
بين مخالب الوجود،
بمدرسة وسطى
بقوة دفع رباعي
تحت حراسة البط،
الإنسان السيزيفي،
القطن،
والحقيقةَ.

– لماذا نُردّد الكلمات؟
– لماذا نكرر الكلمات؟
– اللغة خاوية
– اللغة تعمل

College of Midwifery

Najlaa Osman Eltom
Translated from Arabic by Mayada Ibrahim

One can walk a maze made of a single word,
for fifty years,
or gather firewood from the forest as it snores,
or start a small fire that agitates the midwife,
her cigarette in hand;
her name is Najat.*

Najat, Najat
grew up with domesticated filth-covered ducks,
and trained for midwifery at college.

The college
the college
the maze made of one woman,
rolls like a hedgehog
between claws of existence,
in a middle school
with the force of a truck,
under the watchful eye of the ducks,
the Sisyphean figure,
the cotton,
the truth.

—Why do we repeat words?
—Why do we repeat them?
—Language is vacuous
—Language is at work

---

* In Arabic, "najat" means "refuge" or "survival".

في رحلة التقدم ثمة بوّابات تفتيش إلكترونية
تنفجر تلقائيًا عند دخول المجاز؛
لذلك
لا يمكن السير في متاهة مكوّنة من كلمة واحدة.

لماذا نكرّر الكلمات؟
يد القابلة المتوغّلة في الرحم رفعت شارة النصر
والمنكير المبيّ على السبّابة يخفق مثل قلبٍ صناعيّ:
نجاة
نجاة
نجاة
حتى الموت.

On the path to progress, there are electronic checkpoints
if a metaphor walks through, it bursts into flames
for this reason
one cannot walk in a maze made of one word.

The midwife's hand, deep in the uterus, emerges victorious
the pink nail polish pulses like an artificial heart:
Najat
Najat
Najat
until death.

السّفر عبر الزّمن

لينا خلف تقّاحة

ترجمتها عن الإنكليزية مريم ناجي

نعودُ حتى
تعرفوا مَن كنّا

ومَن كنتم لتكونوا إن
عشتم هنا.

نعود حتى
تتمكنوا من أن تصبحوا ما أنتم عليه.

نحن عائدون ولسنا زائرون

لأنّه حتى في هذه اللحظة
بعد أن عشنا هنا وقتًا أطول

ما عشنا في أيّ مكانٍ آخر
ما زلنا نفكّر في هذا المكان

كمكانٍ جديد، كوجهةٍ،
مثل تيارٍ نغادر به

رحم
الظلمة أو أحضان

المحبة. نعودُ لأنّ
الحركة تَبثُ فينا راحةً أكثر

من الاستقرار، من التصلُّب.
نعودُ لأن هذا يعني

Time Travel

Lena Khalaf Tuffaha

We travel back so that you
will know who we were and who

you might have been if you
had lived here too.

We travel back so that you
can become who you are.

We travel *back* not *to*

because even now
after we've lived longer

here than anywhere else
we still think of this place

as new, as a destination,
a motion forward

out of the womb
of darkness or the arms of

love. We travel because
motion is more comfort

than settling, calcifying.
We travel because it means

أننا لم نَصل بعدُ
إلى حيثُ نحنُ ذاهبون، القصة

لا تزال قيد الكتابة
وعظامنا المكسورةُ لم تُجبر بعد.

ما يزال أمامنا فرصةٌ
لأن يختلف مآلنا

أو أن يتحسَّن أو -في أفضل حال-
أن نُشابه آبائنا دون

أن نعرف أننا غدونا
هم. نسافرُ

لأننا تعرَّفنا على
وِجهتنا حين

رحلنا، وبتكرار الرحيل
وُلدنا ولادةً جديدةً كمهاجرين

درسوا الخريطة،
وتعلَّموا اللغة

فَهِموا إشارات الشوارع
وتقلُّبات الجو. نسافر

لنتتبَّع ألحية الأشجار العتيقة
ونستندُ على جدرانٍ

بلونِ جلودنا، نعود
بالزمن حيثُ العصفور

we haven't gotten to where
we're going yet, the story

is still being written and
our fractures aren't done setting.

There is still a chance
we'll turn out different

or better or—best of all—
like our parents without

knowing we've become
who they were. We travel

because we knew
where we were going when

we left, and leaving again
we are born-again immigrants

who have already studied the map,
learned the language,

can decipher the street signs and
the weather patterns. We travel

to trace the bark of old trees
and lean against walls

the color of our skin, we travel
back to where the bird

الذي يُرفرفُ طائرًا من حناجرنا
حين تغنون أنتم، ويعشِّش

على أغصان شجِرة السرو،
والمربيّتة التي تُهدِّئ

رجفتكم، تنمو في ظلال
ذكرياتكم. نتأرجح

إلى الماضي وإلى الحاضر في هذا
المسار اللولبيّ، قصةٌ تدور

في خصلاتٍ من أشعة الشمس
والأتربة، صفحاتٌ وصفحاتٌ من الترجمة.

that flies out of our throat
when you sing nests

in the cypress branches,
and the sage that soothes your

trembling grows in the shade
of our memories. We travel

back and forward in this
revolution, a story spun

in strands of sunlight and
dust, pages and pages of translation.

غاليلو/لي
سمر دياب

لو أنها تَدورُ، لرأيت بجعَ إنكلترا في حضن طفلٍ يحتضرُ في الصومال،
يضعُ رأسه في فمه ويتوسّل إليه أن يقضمه ...

لو أنها تدور، لكانت دخلتْ نجمةٌ حذائي وأنا أدوس بحقدٍ على السماء وأنظر
إلى جحور النمل فوق رأسي تضيء بسعادة ...

لو أنها تدور،
لما احتجتُ لأن أدير وجهي وأراقب شفاه جارتي الخرساء
لأفهم أنها تقول:la vida es triste

عفواً، أنا هكذا أفهم الدوران ...

لو أنها تدور، لكان البحر الآن في عشّ طائرٍ، فاتحاً فه لِيدخل منقار أمّه
إلى جوفه بحشرةٍ صغيرة، تسدّ جوع السفينة التي ترفسه في بطنه كل يوم ...

لو أنها تدور، لارتدى الدراويش ثيابهم النظيفة، وماتوا واقفين ...

لو أنها تدور، لاكتشفتنا القارّات قبل أن نكتشفها - على الأقل كانت مَشَت
أمريكا إلى كولومبوس وهو رضيع ووضعت وسادةً على وجهه لخمس
دقائق ...

لو أنها تدور، يا عزيزي، لهرهر الموتى من أضرحتهم، وظننّاهم مطرّاً،
وتمشّينا تحتهم نتحدثُ عن الحبّ والرغبة. الصغار منهم رذاذ لطيف
والباقي مطر غزير، وانتظرناهم كلَّ موسم كي لا يفسد المحصول ...

Galeo/li

Samar Diab

Translated from Arabic by Nofel

If it rotated, you would have seen the English pelican in between
the arms of a dying child in Somalia, putting its head in his mouth,
begging him to bite into it ...

If it rotated, a star would have gotten into my shoes as I stomped
on the sky with resentment, looking at anthills above my head,
lighting up joyously ...

If it rotated,
I wouldn't have needed to turn my face and observe my deaf
neighbour's lips to understand that she was saying: la vida es triste.

Pardon me, but that's how I understand rotation ...

If it rotated, the sea would have been in a bird's nest opening its
mouth for its mother's beak to enter its craw with a small insect,
filling the hunger of the ship kicking its belly every day ...

If it rotated, the dervishes would have worn their clean clothes and
died standing ...

If it rotated, continents would have discovered us before we
discovered them—at least then, the Americas would've walked to
Columbus as an infant and placed a pillow over his face for five
minutes ...

If it rotated, my dear,
the dead would've fallen from their shrines like raindrops
and we would've ambled beneath them talking about love and

لو أنها تدور، لفعل الله شيئاً ليوقف هذا الحشد المترنِّح من الكائنات، كان دقَّ مسمارين في يديها، كعادته، وأنهى هذه الفانتازيا المضحكة ...

لو أنها تدور، لماذا هذا الظلّ يتبعني حتى إلى الشعر، حتى إلى الجحيم؟
لو أنها تدور، لماذا الرحم في مكانه، والذاكرة في مكانها، والوردة التي سيأكلها الماعز في مكانها؟

..عفواً ثانيةً، لكني هكذا أفهم الدوران ...

غاليلو/ لي
الأمر ليس كما تظنُّ يا عزيزي
سلامة نظرك
إنها بيضةُ طائرٍ خائفٍ، ليس إلا.

desire. The young a gentle drizzle, the rest a heavy rainfall.
We would've awaited them every season for crops not to rot ...

If it rotated,
God would've done something to stop these masses of wobbling
creatures. He would've nailed both hands as usual, ending this
laughable fantasy ...

If it rotated, then why does this shadow follow me, even to poetry,
even to hell?

Pardon me, again, but that's how I understand rotation ...

Galeo/li
It is not what you think. Not to belittle your vision, but this is the
egg of a terrified bird, nothing else.

ها هي أجراسي

دعد حدّاد

استيقظوا الآن
أنا وحيدةٌ
ها هي أجراسي وتوابيتي
ها هو بساطُ رحمتي الأحمديُّ
ها هو قلبي المفتوحُ
ونوافذي مشرعةٌ
وستارتي مزَّقتها الريحُ
سوداءُ سوداءُ بَشَرتي
وعيوني آه
وثيابي مهلهلةٌ كالدُّرِّ
وقدماي عاريتان
من قلّة الخجل

١٦ آذار ١٩٨٩

72

Here are My Bells

Daad Haddad

Translated from Arabic by Rana Issa and Suneela Mubayi

Wake up now,
I am alone.
Here are my bells and my coffins,
here on my rug I offer mercy for all.
Here is my open heart,
my windows agape,
my curtains ripped apart by the wind.
Black, so black is my skin
and my eyes, oh god.
My clothes tattered
like scattered pearls,
and my feet bare
from lack of shame.

March 16th, 1989

ماءٌ وملح

لينا خلف تفّاحة

ترجمتها عن الإنكليزية مريم ناجي

خلف جدران سجونك ننتظر
دقّات قلبٍ مسموعةٍ، جلجلةٍ مكتومة
أعلى تيار الدم المتدفق نحيلًا
نهيراتٌ نيليةُ الزُرقة تنبض صاخبةً أسفل الجلد الرقيق
جافًا وخشنًا كالجدران الحجرية التي تسوّرنا.

نستلقي جنبًا إلى جنب،
جوعى لِما لا يسده طعام،

نحفر مأوًى
لا يهدُّه أي قصف،
ولا تترك غُرف التحقيق فيه نُدبةً

هذا ألمنا   نحن مَن نقرر
كيف نعيش وإن مِتنا
نحن نقرر   مَن يُعطي ومن يأخذ

نحن نطالب بحرّيّتنا

لتحويل الحجارة إلى شمسٍ تتسلل إلى سجونكم
لارتشاف الماء والملح مثل طقسٍ مقدّس

حرّيّتنا

لامتلاك أجسادنا والأرض التي تحتها
لاستنشاق الهواء على جانبي الجدار

حرّيّتنا

74

Water and Salt

Lena Khalaf Tuffaha

Behind the walls of your jails we wait
heartbeats audible now, muffled thuds
above the current of blood running thin
indigo rivulets pulsing loud beneath parchment skin
chafing and coarse like stone walls that surround us.

We lie side to side,
we hunger for what eating cannot feed,

we carve out a sanctuary
that no beating can tear down,
no interrogation room scars can pierce

this is our ache   we decide
how we live and if we die
we decide   who gives and who takes away

we claim the freedom

to turn stone into sunlight streaming through your jails
to sip water and salt like sacrament

freedom

to own our bodies and the land beneath them
to breathe the air on both sides of the wall

freedom

لأن ننتظر وننتظر
عند نقاط تفتيشكم وأبراج مراقبتكم
حتى تبتلعكم موجةٌ ساحقة

من الماء والملح
لم تتوقعوا قدومها لحظةً، لحظة الصفاء هذه
وكيف أصبحنا كلّ هذا المحيط.

to wait and wait
for your checkpoints and your watchtowers
to be subsumed in a crashing wave

of water and salt
you never saw it coming, this cleansing,
how we have become this ocean.

رجل وحيد يمشي على الجسر
سمر دياب

كان يقصّ سيرته على امرأة جميلة في بيته
قال
كنتُ أمشي كثيرًا وحيدًا على الجسر
أفكّر بطائرٍ بارد
بريشٍ بارد وعيونٍ باردة
يموت أمام النافذة
كنتُ أبتسم مثل صدع في الهواء الذي يسوق الخريف إلى الأحياء
والصيف إلى الأمواتِ
وأبكي مثل أحذية فارغة
فكّرت كثيرًا بالرحم الذي عشت فيه حياة سعيدة
حيث لا ريح تخلع قبّعتي
حيث لا أحد يدقّ الباب
ووددتُ لو أعود لأتكوّر هناك
أنا وقبّعتي وكلبي وإبريق الشاي الساخن
كنت أمشي وحدي دون شهوة ودون ذاكرة
دون أن أجفل حين يدهس القطار البحيرة
أو يسرقني أحد المشردين
أصل إلى نهاية الجسر، ثم أعود أدراجي
وأفكّر في طريق العودة
لماذا كلّ هذا الوخز في قلبي
أنا الذي لا أريد شيئًا

78

A Lonely Man Walks on the Bridge

Samar Diab

Translated from Arabic by Nofel

He was recounting his story to a beautiful woman at his house.
He said:
I used to walk alone on the bridge a lot
thinking of a cold bird
with cold feathers and cold eyes
dying in front of the window.
I used to smile like a rift in the wind, blowing fall to the living
and summer to the dead
and I used to weep like empty shoes.
I thought a lot about the womb in which I lived a joyous life
where no wind takes off my hat
where no one knocks on the door
and I wished to return to curl up there,
me and my hat and my dog and the hot tea pot.
I used to walk alone without lust, without memory,
without flinching at the train trampling the lake
or a homeless person stealing from me.
I used to reach the end of the bridge and then return
and think on the way back:
Why does my heart sting this much,
I, who want nothing?

أبو ناصر

لينا خلف تفّاحة

ترجمتها عن الإنكليزية مريم ناجي

سجّادة صلاةٍ خفيفةٌ ورثّة
تفصلُ أبو ناصر عن الأرض الترابية.
ساقاه مطويتان تحته،
وعيناه مصوبتان نحو المدخل
تتجاوزان المدى أمامه،
خلف جدول المجاري الرفيع
المُنساب على الطريق
رائحةٌ كريهةٌ تخيّم على حرارة يوليو،
ذبابٌ يطنّ عاليًا في سحبٍ كثيفة.

في غرفته المعتمة، أبو ناصر
يداوي التهاب مفاصله وحنينه.
لا أحد يأتي بشايه في الظهيرة
أو يطّمئنُ على مفاصله المتورمة،
أو يعدّلُ الوسادة خلف ظهره.
تخلّى عن مسبحته
حين آلت جثتها إلى
صمت مقبرة المخيّم الصارخ.

جميلةٌ كما في أوّل يومٍ قبّلها،
جبينها لمسهُ مرةً قُبيل
أن يكفّنوها بالكتان الأبيض
ويحملوها بعيدًا.
الآن في عتمة النهار في غرفته،
الصورة الأخيرة المحفورة في ذاكرته
كانت شاهد قبرها المتواضع—
أم ناصر، ١٩٣٩-٢٠٠٥
مواليد حيفا، فلسطين.

Abu Nasser

Lena Khalaf Tuffaha

A thin and tattered prayer rug
separates Abu Nasser from the dirt floor.
Legs folded under him,
his eyes face the doorway
looking beyond the road outside,
past the thin stream of sewage
trickling down the road,
stench hanging low in July heat,
flies buzzing overhead in the thick clouds.

In his dark room Abu Nasser
nurses arthritis and longing.
No one brings tea in the afternoon
or asks after his swollen joints,
adjusts the cushion at the small of his back.
He gives up his prayer beads
when her body descends into
the deep-throated silence of the camp graveyard.

Beautiful as the first day he kissed her,
her forehead he touches once before
they wrap her in white linen
and carry her away.
Now in the daytime darkness of his room,
the last sight seared into memory
her modest headstone—
Um Nasser, 1939-2005
Born in Haifa, Palestine.

سجادة صلاةٍ خفيفةٌ ورثَّة
تفصلُ أبو ناصر عن الأرض الترابية.
أصوات المخيّم تصدحُ خارج غرفته
خشخشة أخبار اليوم على الراديو
كلها رموزٌ ملغَزة.
مستوطنون انسحاب جيش مفاوضات
تطنُّ بصخبٍ فوق رأسه.

A thin and tattered prayer rug
separates Abu Nasser from the dirt floor.
The sounds of the camp beyond his room
crackle of the day's news on the radio .
all indecipherable syllables.
settlers   withdrawal   army   negotiations
buzzing loudly overhead.

طعام رأسي
قاسم سعودي

في بيتها القديم
كانت أختي تطعم العقارب
مخافةَ أن تلدغَ أطفالَها
مثلما أفعل
أطعمكِ رأسي
حتّى لا يصاب العشّاق بالخيبة
الشهداء بالذعر
والمدينة بالشّياطين.

I Feed You My Head

Qasim Saudi

Translated from Arabic by Ibrahim Fawzy

In her old house,
my sister fed the scorpions
fearing they would sting her children.
I do the same.
I feed you my head
so that lovers suffer no disappointment,
martyrs feel no terror,
and the city is not struck by demons.

يمشي وحيدًا
قاسم سعودي

في المقبرة
قالت العجوز لماذا يمشي وحيدًا هذا القبر
أجاب الولد: هذا ليس قبرًا
يا أمي
هذا أبي يتعقّب الشهداء كل ليلة

Walking Alone

Qasim Saudi

Translated from Arabic by Ibrahim Fawzy

In the cemetery,
the old woman asked why this grave walks alone.
The boy replied: *This is not a grave, Mother,*
this is my father, tracking the martyrs every night.

زيارةُ النَّهرِ

علي محمود خضير

تَروقُني زيارةُ النهرِ ليلًا
لا أخشى الظلمةَ
ولستُ محظوظًا برؤيةِ الأشباح
الموجاتُ وئيدةً تقطعُ بعضها
وتدخلُ في قلبي
فانوسٌ يَترنّحُ في الضفةِ الأخرى
نميمُ جُرذٍ بين القصبات
وقاربٌ يثقبُهُ الماءُ .

إن كانت الأسماكُ تلبطُ تحتَ الشطِ
فهي تلبطُ في رأسي أيضًا
وعلى قميصي رائحةُ مراكبَ ضَليلة.

*

هذا الليل يُربكني
أكنتُ رجلًا يزورُ نهرًا في ليلٍ
أم أنا النهر؟

أنا عليلُ الوحدةِ الذي
لا يُشفى
ولا يمُوت .

The Tigris Visitor

Ali Mahmoud Khudayyir

Translated from Arabic by Zeena Faulk

I like to visit the river at night—
darkness doesn't frighten me,
nor am I fortunate enough to see ghosts.
Sombre river waves slowly cut through each other,
and enter my core.
A lantern falters on the other bank,
a rat bustles among the reeds,
and the torrent pierces a quffa.

If fish squirm beneath the shore,
in my head, too, they squirm, and
on my shirt lingers a wandering vessel's scent.

*

The night confuses me—
Was I a man visiting the river at night?
Or was I the river?

I am sick with loneliness—
neither recuperating
nor dying.

أكتب عصفورًا وأقصد جثة المنزل
قاسم سعودي

أكتبُ عصفورًا وأقصدُ جثّة المنزل
أكتب غرفة وأقصدُ درّاجة الهواء
أكتبُ مسجدًا وأقصدُ تلك الفتاة الطويلة التي تلتقطُ
الفاكهة التالفة من أرض السوق
أكتبُ وردة وأقصد لا شيء
لا شيء تمامًا
لا شيء مثلك
وأنت تقف عاريًا أمام المرآة
والحشرات تخرج من جسدك
لكن
ثمة رأسٌ يُطلّ من الفم ويخبرُني
ما رأيكَ ببعض الشاي الآن
بعض الشاي فقط
بعض الشاي.

I Write Sparrow and Mean the House Corpse

Qasim Saudi

Translated from Arabic by Ibrahim Fawzy

I write sparrow and mean the corpse of the house.
I write room and mean bicycle.
I write mosque and mean that tall girl who
picks spoiled fruit from the market ground
I write rose and mean nothing,
nothing at all.
Nothing, just like yourself,
as you stand naked before a mirror
with insects crawling out of you.
But then
a head pops out of the mouth to tell me:
How about some tea now?
Just some tea,
Some tea.

طرق العيش صعبة
عمر الجفّال

نحن عاديّون
حتّى أننا نستطيع البكاء
على كتف نملةٍ جائعة،
أو ندلّ الغربان
على جدول جثث طويل
لتعلّمنا الدفن مجددًا.

وربما نرافق غزلانًا
في البريّات
لنقفز الحدود،
أو لننتحر معها على الطرقات السريعة.

ومن يدري،
أن بعد كل الذي جرى ... بعد كل الذي سيجري
أن بإمكاننا الطيران
إلى السماوات
بخفّة صقر
دون أن نترك
ريشةً واحدة كأثرٍ
على وجودنا.

The Living is Hard

Omar Aljaffal

Translated from Arabic by Yasmine Haj

We are so ordinary
that we could cry
on a hungry ant's shoulder,
or guide the crows
to a long stream of corpses
to teach us again how to bury.

We might even escort gazelles
in the wilderness
to jump borders,
or take our own lives, as they do, on motorways.

And who could have known,
after all that has happened ... after all that will,
that we could fly
to the heavens
with the lightness of a falcon
leaving behind
not one feather to show
for our existence.

رمادي فاتح

علي محمود خضير

أرتجفُ الآنَ
كأنِّي غصنٌ خفيفٌ في عاصفة
أو ورقةٌ تريدُ أن تمْلأَ بأيِّ شيءٍ
سوى أن تكونَ وحيدةً على الطَّاولة.

أسألُ :
كم مشت الأيام؟
كم ابتعدنا عن البدايةِ؟
هل بدأنا؟

أُديرُ كأس ترابٍ يدعونهُ العُمر :
ما علاجُ الفقد يا صديقُ؟

وإذْ أجلسُ على كرسيٍّ
آخرَ الغرفةِ الباردةِ
أقولُ :
سأنسى
كلَّ من تذكَّروني لأنهم شعروا بالوحدة
وكلَّ من نسُوني لأنهم لم يعودوا وحيدين.

أقولُ،
وأنظرُ لساعةِ الجدارِ،
مُرتجفًا
كأنِّي غصنٌ
أُريدَ لهُ،
أن يكونَ وحيدًا
في العاصفة.

Light Grey

Ali Mahmoud Khudayyir

Translated from Arabic by Zeena Faulk

Trembling now
      like a delicate bough in a windstorm,
or a blank paper that yearns to be filled with anything—
      than be left alone on a desk.

I wonder
      how far the days have drifted by,
      and how far we've moved from the starting line.
      I wonder whether we have even started.

I turn over the hourglass they call our life.
      How could a loss be made whole, oh friend?

As I sit down on a chair
at the back of an empty room,
I say,
          I'll forget
      those who remembered me because of their loneliness,
      and those who forgot me, because they're no longer alone.

I utter verse,
as I glance at the clock.
      Trembling,
      like a bough
      fated
      to be alone
      in the windstorm.

حرب
war

Privilege and context choose our battles as we articulate their time span, and translate their fronts. A new front opens when its predecessor decides that translation will no longer suffice in the process of decolonizing a mind, a body, and its lands—only the mother tongue will.

Translation must hold still sometimes, be a silent observer of indecipherable warriors.

الفولغا الصفراء
نجلاء عثمان التّوم

في الثمانينات
امتلك أبي سيارة فولغا روسية.
وعلى طريق الكدرو،
ذات يوم،
احترقت الماكينة بوقار.
لكن روسيا استمرت؛
جلست معنا، في فستان الدمورية المدرسي،
نحن بنات الصحافة زلط
وقالت التضاريس؛
حفظناها عن ظهر قلب
خوفًا من الجلد،
حفظنا محطات قطار فلادفستك
محطة محطّة،
وذات يوم احترقت تلك المحطات
بهدوء
ولم نعرها أي اهتمام.
الحرب الباردة لم تكن باردة أو ساخنة
كانت مسلّية،
وعلى طريق الكدرو
تعانقت أشجار النيم
ورقصت حول الصفيح السوفيتي
رقصة الزمن.

Yellow Volga

Najlaa Osman Eltom

Translated from Arabic by Mayada Ibrahim

In the eighties,
my father owned a Russian Volga.
One day,
on Kadaro Street,
the engine burned with dignity.
But Russia went on;
it sat with us,
the girls of Sahafa Street,
in a cotton school uniform.
It said that
we knew by heart
the ground elevations
out of fear of punishment.
It asked about the route of the Vladivostok train,
which we had memorised,
station by station.
One day, these stations burned
quietly
and we paid them no mind.
The Cold War was neither cold nor hot;
it was entertaining.
On Kadaro Street,
the neem trees embraced
and danced around the Soviet tin sheets
the dance of time.

إلى مقاتل في الجبهة

لميعة عباس عمارة

وأيقظني البرد في أخريات ليالي الخريف
تَلَمَّتُ
راحت ذراعي تَجسُ مكانَكَ
عادت تُجمِّع حولي دثاري الخفيف.
مكانك لا ههنا ...
قد تذكرتُ
أنت رحلت مع الجيش أمس
أراك، ومُتربةٌ جبهة الفارس العربي
وصوت القذائف يشحنه بالرجولة
غدًا سأعانق فيك البطولة
غفرتُ لبردِ ليالي الخريف
ووحشة تلك الليالي الطويلة

غدًا سألتمع نجماتك الشامخات
على كتفٍ يشهدُ الزهو أنّي أشدُّ
عليها
وتحسدُني مائة امرأة
ألا احسدنَّني
إنني
أعانقه ...
عانقَ الهولَ لم يرتعش جفنه
وَرَدَ لهيب المنايا إليها

وديعًا بصدري يغمر عينيه
مرتعشًا
ما ألذَّ ...
فديت البطولة
كم مقتحمٌ عبقريٌّ لديها!

100

To a Fighter on the Frontlines

Lamia Abbas Amara

Translated from Arabic by Hiba Moustafa

The cold awakened me in the last of autumn nights.
I curled up.
My arm reached out to feel for your place,
then back to gather the light blanket around me.
You are not here ...
I now remember:
yesterday, you left with the army.
I see you, with the dusty forehead of an Arab horseman,
the sound of missiles charging his manliness.
Tomorrow, I will embrace the valour in you
and forgive the cold of autumn nights
and their loneliness.

Tomorrow, I will polish your towering accolades
on a shoulder I pride myself in holding,
and a hundred women will envy me.
Oh, do envy me
for I am
embracing him ...
He embraced horror, his eyelids never quivered,
and paid fate its blaze back.

Gently, he buries his face in my breasts
shivering
how delightful ...
Valour
has never known
a valiant genius like you!

دمهم

إبراهيم نصر الله

دمُهم صباحُ الخيرْ
دمهم مساءُ الخيرْ
دمهم تحيّتُهم ... رسالتُهم إلينا
دمهم حكايتُهم ... وخوفهم علينا
دمهمِ مساجدُهم ... كنائسُهمْ
نوافذُ دورهمْ
دمهم محبّتُهم وغضبتُهم
دمهم عتابٌ جارحٌ
دمهم فضاءٌ فاضحٌ
دمهم حكايةُ أمّهمْ لصغارِها
دمهم رسالةُ وردةٍ لرحيقها
دمهم طيورُ بلادهم ورياحُها
دمهم معاركُهم ...وهدنتُهم
وطرفتُهم إذا اندفَع الغزاةُ
دمهم ذراعُ صلاتِهمْ
دمهم صلاةٌ

لم يتركوا شجرًا يعاتبهم
ولا قمرًا على شرفاتِ منزلهمْ
ولا أغنيةً عطشى لأنهرهمْ
لم يكسروا أُمنيةً سكنتْ عيونَ صغارهمْ
أو خاطرَ الزيتون فوق تلالِهم
هُمْ أصدقاء البحر
هم أصدقاءُ النهْر
هم أعينُ الزيتونْ
هم زهرةُ الحنّونْ
هم خُضرةُ الأشجارْ
وطفولةُ الأنهارْ
هم قِبلةُ الشعراءْ

Their Blood

Ibrahim Nasrallah

Translated from Arabic by Eman Abukhadra

Their blood is good morning,
their blood is good night.
It is their greeting ... their message to us
their tale ... and their fear for us.
Their blood is their mosques ... their churches,
windows to their homes,
their love and their anger,
a piercing reproach,
a scandalous space,
a mother's tale to her children,
a rose's message to its nectar,
their land's birds and its winds.
Their blood is their battles ... and their truce,
their quip, should the invaders storm in.
It is an arm for their prayers
and a prayer is their blood.

They left no trees to reproach them,
nor a moon over their balconies,
nor a song thirsty for their rivers.
They broke no wish dwelling in their children's eyes,
nor the spirit of olive trees over their hills.
They are friends of the sea,
friends of the river,
the eyes of olive trees,
the anemone flower,
the greenness of trees,
and the childhood of rivers.
They are a Mecca for poets

وذخيرةُ الفقراءْ
هم شارعٌ في الفجرْ
هم ضحكةٌ في الصخرْ
ووضوحُ هذا السّرْ
دمهم صباحُ الخير
دمهم مساءُ الخير

and a reserve for the poor,
a road at dawn,
a laugh within the rocks,
and the clarity of this secret.
Their blood is good morning,
their blood is good night.

أنا من تحمل الزهور إلى قبرها
دعد حدّاد

أنا ابنة الشيطان
أنا ابنة هذه الليلة المجنونة
ابنة وعيي
وصديقي ... أنا
أنا أكثرُ الناس عِثقًا
أنا خمري من شراييني
أنا من تحمل الزهور إلى قبرها،
وتبكي ... من شِدَّة الشعر

الواحدة والنصف من ليل ١٧-١٨ آذار

I Am the One Who Brings Flowers to Her Grave

Daad Haddad

Translated from Arabic by Rana Issa and Suneela Mubayi

I am the devil's daughter
I am the daughter of this frenzied night
the daughter of my consciousness
and my own friend.
I am the most antique of people,
wine runs in my veins.
I am she
who brings flowers to her grave*
and weeps from the pull of poetry

1:30am, March 17-18

---

* Syrian filmmaker Hala Abdallah used this famous line from Haddad's poem as
the title of her 2006 auto-documentary.

مثل قارب خشبيٍّ مقلوبٍ في الصحراء
قاسم سعودي

مثل قارب خشبيٍّ مقلوبٍ في الصحراء
أنامُ على السقف
يصرخ السائق العجوز
"استيقظوا أيها الشجعان
لقد وصلنا إلى الجنة."
نحملُ بنادقَنا
ونركض
ياه كم هو لذيذ أن تُطلق الرصاص
على رأس أحدهم ...

Like an Upside-Down Boat in the Desert

Qasim Saudi

Translated from Arabic by Ibrahim Fawzy

Like an upside-down wooden boat in the desert,
I lie adrift
on the deck.
The old driver yells,
> *Wake up, brave ones,*
> *we've reached paradise.*
Carrying our rifles, running.
Oh, how sweet it is to fire a bullet
> into somebody's head ...

ربما في كوكب آخر
قاسم سعودي

١

أجِدُني طائرًا سعيدًا
أو يتيمًا
أو بلا جناح
لا بأس
لكن ماذا يفعل هذا هنا؟
القتّاصُ الذي يطارِدُني من كوكبٍ لآخر

٢

يجلسُ في الطابق العلوي
ينفخ في المزمار
تخرجُ الحروب تباعًا
ينظر إلينا بحزن وهو يدخّن وحدته
ثم يرمي على ما تبقى منّا شيئًا يُسمى الحبّ
هكذا يواصل الجنود حياتهم
هكذا نواصل حياتنا أيضًا
بالقليلِ من الحبّ
والكثير من الكراهية.

٣

مثل أشياءٍ فائضة عن الحاجة
يرمون بنا من الأعالي
يبتسمون كثيرًا
ونحن نسقط
الآن نحن نصطدم بالأرض
ثم نتوزع
على هيئة جنود

Perhaps on Some Other Planet

Qasim Saudi

Translated from Arabic by Ibrahim Fawzy

1

I find myself a happy bird
or orphaned
or wingless.
        Not to worry,
But, what is this one doing here?
This sniper chases me from one planet to another.

2

He sits in the attic,
blowing his flute.
Wars turn up in succession.
He gazes at us sadly,
smoking his loneliness,
then throws onto what remains of us
something called love.
This is how soldiers resume life.
This is how we do, too.
With little love,
and much hate.

3

Like superfluous objects,
they cast us from above.
Their smiles abundant,
as we plummet.
Now we crash into the earth's unyielding ground,
then disperse, transforming into soldiers of war.

٤

عن الطريقة الأمثل لقتل طائر في السماء
صوِّب بشكل جيد
اضغط على الزناد برشاقة
انتظر لحظة
ها هو الدم ينزل من رأسك
هل أنت سعيد الآن؟
حسنًا
اقتل الرجل الذي بقربك

4

The best way to kill a flying bird:
Take careful aim, with precision and poise.
Press the trigger swiftly.
Wait a moment.
Now, blood trickles down over your head.
Happy now?
Very well,
kill the man beside you.

هذا الكوكب الأرضي
فدوى طوقان

لو بِيَدي
لو أنّي أقدرُ أن أقلبَهُ هذا الكوكب
أن أُفرغَهُ من كلّ شُرور الأرض
أن أقتلعَ جذورَ البُغض
لو أنّي أقدرُ، لو بِيَدي
أن أقصي قابيلَ التَّغلب
أقصيهِ إلى أبعدِ كوكب
أن أغسلَ بالماءِ الصّافي
إخوةَ يوسف
وأُطهّرَ أعماقَ الإخوة
من دَنَسِ الشّرّ.
لو بِيَدي
أن أمسحَ عن هذا الكوكبْ
بَصماتِ الفقر
وأحرّره من أسرِ القهر
لو أنّي أقدرُ لو بِيَدي
أن أجتثَّ جذورَ الظّلم
وأُجفّفه هذا الكوكب
من أنهار الدّم
لو أني أملكُ، لو بِيَدي
أن أرفعَ للإنسانِ المُتعب
في دربِ الحيرةِ والأحزانْ
قنديلَ رخاءٍ واطمئنانْ
أن أمنحَهُ العيشَ الآمن
لو أنّي أقدرُ، لو بِيَدي
لكن ما بِيَدي شيءٌ إلّا لكن
لو أنّي أملكُ أن أملأَ هذا الكوكب
بِبُذور الحُبّ
فتعرّشُ في كلّ الدّنيا

114

This Earthly Planet

Fadwa Tuqan

Translated from Arabic by Eman Abukhadra

I wish it were in my hands,
I wish I could flip this planet,
empty it from the evils of Earth,
and pluck the roots of hate.
I wish I could, I wish it were in my hands
to banish the sly Cain,
banish him to the farthest of planets,
and wash with pure water
the siblings of Joseph,
to purify their depths
from the impurities of evil.
I wish it were in my hands
to wipe off this planet
the imprints of poverty
and free it from the captivity of oppression.
I wish I could, I wish it were in my hands
to uproot injustice
and dry the rivers of blood
off of this planet.
I wish I could, I wish it were in my hands,
to hold for the man, tired
in the path of confusion and sorrow,
a lamp of prosperity and serenity
and grant him a safe life.
I wish I could, I wish it were in my hands,
yet all I have at hand is a 'but'.
I wish I were able to fill this planet
with seeds of love
so that the whole world is embowered

أشجارُ الحُبّ
ويصيرُ الحبُّ هو الدّنيا
ويصيرُ الحبُّ منارَ الدّرب.
لو بِيَدي أن أحمَيهُ هذا الكوكب
من شرّ خيارٍ صَعبْ
لو بِيَدي
أن أرفعَ عن هذا الكوكبِ
كابوسَ الحَربْ!

in trees of love,
and love becomes the world
and lights the path.
I wish I could protect this planet
from the evils of a hard decision.
I wish I could
rid this planet
of the nightmare of war!

مجاهيل

علي محمود خضير

السَّيارةُ المجهولة
تدخلُ شارعاً لا اسمَ له
يترجَّلُ مجهولون
بأيديهم آلاتٌ مُبهمة
صليلٌ سريعٌ
تَجفلُ العصافيرُ والأرواحُ ...
يسقطُ رجلٌ مجهولٌ
سريعًا إلى الأرض؛
الأرضُ التي نجهلُ اسمها
إلى الآن ...

Unknowns

Ali Mahmoud Khudayyir

Translated from Arabic by Zeena Faulk

The unknown car
arrived on a nameless street.
Unknown men get out,
clutching obscure machine guns.
A swift clatter so loud,
sparrows and souls flinch ...
An unknown man falls,
abruptly onto the ground;
the ground whose name
is unknown to us still ...

أطفئوا هذه النّار

نور بعلوشة

هذه النار العالية مَنْ وزّع عليها لحمنا؟
مَنْ قال للريح أنّنا أوراق؟
مَنْ قال للحزن أنّنا الخريف؟
مَنْ قال للحياة أنّنا قطع دومينو؟
مَنْ لعِب في القصّة؟
مَنْ قال إنّ الأطفال يموتون؟
وكيف يموت الأطفال؟

رائحة الشوكولا الّتي تملأ الدنيا
هذا الشفق المستمرّ
هذه الأحلام الّتي تسقط من السماء
رائحة الياسمين الّتي تلمع
أصوات الأطفال الّذين كانوا مثل النمل يركضون على بوابات المدارس
الشوارع الّتي تبكي طيلة الوقت
البيوت الّتي عاشت عمرًا طويلًا تسبح في القصص
ماذا حصل لها حتّى نامت هكذا؟
كيف تنام البيوت على أصحابها وتكسّر عظمهم؟
كيف حصلت هذه الخيانة؟
كيف يسقط السقف على عيونٍ ذابت فيه لأعوامٍ وأعوام؟

كيف انشقّ الشارع؟
كيف صار رملًا هكذا؟

كيف انهارت المدرسة؟
كيف صار كلّ هذا الدم؟

ما هذه الرائحة؟
كيف خانتنا؟
كيف وقفت هكذا مبتعدة؟

120

Quench This Fire

Nour Balousha

Translated from Arabic by Nashwa Nasreldin

Who laid our flesh over this ravenous fire?
Who told the wind that we were leaves?
Who told melancholy that we were autumn?
Who told life that we were domino tiles?
Who tampered with the story?
Who said that children were dying?
How do children die?

The heady aroma of chocolate
this constant twilight
these dreams that drop from the sky
the glittering scent of jasmine
the squeals of little ones, who used to stream like ants at school gates
the ever-weeping streets
the homes that for years waded through stories.
What happened to make them slumber in this manner?
How could they lay across their owners and crush their bones?
How could this betrayal occur?
How could a ceiling crumble onto eyes that for years stared into it?

How did the road cleave?
And resurrect as sand?

How did the school collapse?
From where did all this blood appear?

What is that smell?
How did it betray us?
Why does it keep its distance?

أين أطباق الأُمّهات؟
أين رائحة الغسيل والسقاقية والرمّانيّة والسلطة الحارّة؟
أين الرائحة؟

ما هذه الخيام؟
ماهي لغتها؟
كيف نتحدّث إليها؟
كيف نرتّب موعدًا حقيقيًّا للفهم؟

كيف جفّ الماء؟
كيف انقطعت الاتصالات؟
كيف نبكي؟
لماذا لا نبكي؟
هل نحن دمعةٌ بالأساس؟

Where are the mothers' dishes?
Where is the smell of laundry, the sumaqiyya, rumaniyya, spicy salad?
Where are all the smells?

What are these tents?
What language do they speak?
How can we communicate with them?
Can we schedule an appointment to understand?

How did the water dry up?
How were communications cut?
How does one cry?
Why don't we cry?
Are we, essentially, a teardrop?

الضّوء الأخضر
كمال ناصر

وسرتُ في مدينة الأموات ...
أدوسُ فوق ظلّي
أسائل الخرائب القتيلة الحياة
عن وطني وأهلي ...
فهالني السكوت والسبات
وهالني الشحوب مدّ ظله، كأنه الرفات ...
يضمني ...
يلفّني ... إذا مشيتُ في مدينة الأموات

*

لا ...
لم أجئ لأمنح الحياة،
مدينتي، ولم أجئ لأجمع الشتات
الجولة الكبرى هوت ...
في ملعب الفوات
وقد أقام الخزي في مأتمها الصلاة ...
مائدة الصراع عهّرت ...
عهّرها الدعاة ...
والرعاة ...
وانتصبت هزيلة ... تطلّ بالفتات ...
لن يشبع الفتات ...
لن يشبع الفتات ...

*

124

The Green Light

Kamal Nasser

Translated from Arabic by Rana Issa

I walk through the city of the dead
trampling over my shadow
I beg the slain ruins for life
in my land and my people.
This silence, this slumber terrifies me
how the pale casts its long shadow, it frightens me, as if it's all
that remains
of the corpses
embracing me
coiling around me ... should I walk in the city of the dead

*

No
I did not come to bring life,
to my city, and I did not come to re-member the fragments.
The big game collapsed
in the playing fields of the endgame
Shame offered prayers at the funeral.
      The banquet of conflict is whored
      made wanton by the propagandists
      and the patrons.
Feeble she stood erect ... bringing crumbs

Crumbs will not satisfy
Crumbs will not satisfy

*

وعندما مشيت في مدينة الأموات ...
أدوس فوق ظلي ...
وأسأل الخرائب القتيلة الحياة،
عن وطني وأهلي ...
وجدت كل شيء ... مات ...

*

وبينما أسير في مدينة الأموات
يقتلني الظّنا ...
تجرحني الـ"أنا ... "
وكبرياء العجز، فاته في موكبي النجاة
لمحت طيفًا يهتك الفنا ...
يدبُّ كالسنا على الدنى
ألفيتُ نفسي أعبر الفلاة ...
أمشي خلفه ...
ألفيتُ نفسي أعبر الحياة ...
أسيرُ كالإيمان، في مدينة الأموات ...
أجيش بالوجود والمنى ...
لمحت طفلًا.. عمره سنة.

١٩٦٥ / ١٠ / ١٥

When I walk in the city of the dead
trampling over my shadow
I beg the slain ruins for life
in my land and my people
I find everything. Died.

*

And when I walked through the city of the dead
desolation killing me
my I wounding me
proud impotence marching away from survival, with me in procession
I caught a spectre obliterating the emptiness
creeping like light on the world.
I found myself traversing the vast expanse
walking behind it.
I found myself crossing through life
walking like faith itself, in the city of the dead ...
the torment of existence surging through me
I glimpsed a child ... one year old.

October 15, 1965*

---

* In this poem, Nasser depicts the harrowing silence following a genocidal storm
in an unnamed city. Unusually for him, he dated the poem. This led me to inquire
whether any lesser known massacre corresponded with the date—I found none.
Was he referring to what he witnessed during the massacre and annihilation of
Palestinian cities in 1948? Or was he seeing into the future, and our present—of
how the city of his birth was to be rendered a city of the dead?

مذكّرات ميدانيّة عن الإرهاب والبدايات

جورج إبراهيم

ترجمته عن الإنكليزيّة نورة الخراشي

في الصورة - أي صورة - الفلسطيني ميت. في الخلفية، حقلٌ من صخورٍ كانت منازل، حقلٌ من الزهور المتساقطة. ما بعد الصورة، يموت الفلسطيني أيضًا. وفي مكانٍ آخر، يموت مرّة أخرى. يُشهَد الفلسطيني ميتًا، وهذه الشهادة، نوعٌ من الموت. طفلٌ لأحدٍ، شقيقٌ لأحدٍ، عزيزٌ على أحد. ملكية الجسد الفلسطيني، وما تبقى من صورته، نوعٌ آخرٌ من الموت. تداول الصُّورَة إلغَاءٌ مُزدَوَج للمِلكيّةِ. ما هو لَنا، كما يُصَوِّرُهُ إحساسُ انفصالِ الجَسَدِ عنِ الأرضِ، علَى فَرضِ أنّنا أحياءٌ، لا يُمكِنُ أن يَكونَ لَنا. ما يُعَدُّ لَنا يَنطوي على نوعٍ من الفَناء، وانعِدامُ الملكيّةِ الّذي يَفرِضُهُ عَيشُنا يَتَجَلَّى كَموتٍ آخرَ. تَداوُلُ الصُّورَةِ بحَرَكةٍ ذَاتِ فَراغٍ في مَركَزِهَا، ينبض. فَراغٌ يَقُولُ: أنظُرْ إلَيَّ، وَيَتَعَفَّنُ عِندَ اللَا-نَظرٍ. فَراغٌ نَقيضُ الصُّورَةِ، وَمَا يَأتي بَعدَ صَوتٍ. لَيسَ منفصلاً عن/ الجسد، إنّما هُوَ الـ'/' مَا بَينَهُمَا. يموت الفلسطيني في الصورة، وأمامها، في أيّ صورة. يموت الفلسطيني في الصورة والحجَر في اليد. يموت الفلسطيني في الصورة والسقف يشتعل. يموت الفلسطيني على المروج مستحيلة الاخضرار. يموت الفلسطيني في الأنقاض، وكأنَّه أنقاض. في الصورة، سياسة التأثير العمودي. تحتَ حامض المستوطن. تحتَ مطر المستوطن. في أيّ صورة. يَموتُ الفِلَسطينيُّ عَلَى الشَّاشَةِ. الهاتفُ الذَّكي مُشحُونٌ بحَامِضِ المَوْتِ. في خلفية الصورة، مراهقٌ، شارةٌ مكونة من ثلاثة حروف على صدره، رشاشٌ موجهٌ نحو الله، يبتسم نحو الشمس، الغاربة فوق أفق جثة فلسطينية. في الصورة، بحر يحمرُّ الأمريكيّ، معتقدًا أننا جميعًا شظايا صغيرة من نفس الضوء النجمي مبتور الأطراف، يفرك وجهه بموتنا والمحيط، ليلتقط صورةً ويسميها حق الولادة. أوروبيّ يحفر وَ... ثمة بلدٌ. الغَرب يُشَارِك الصُّورَة. وَبَعدَهَا، لَا يُوجَدُ بَعْد. إنَّهُ عام ٢٠٢٢. غربًا، تُشَارَك الصُّورَة. الصُّورَةُ، التي فُهِمَت خَطأً أنها حصارٌ إمبرياليٌّ على أوكرانيا، تثيرُ تثير غضبًا يجتاح ما بعد الأمّة. الصُّورَةُ هِيَ صُورَةٌ فِلَسطينيّةٌ، كما تُوَضِّحُ الأسوشيتد برس. تَموتُ الصُّورَةُ مَرَّةً أُخرَى عند عدم تمييزها. الفلسطينيون الأحياء يَموتُونَ في المرآةِ المشَوَّهَةِ لدَورةِ الصُّورَةِ العَفِنَةِ. الفلسطينيون يَموتُونَ في حَياتِهِم. فشَلُ هذه الأرشيفات البصرية هو نوعٌ من الموت. عينٌ

Field Notes on Terror & Beginnings

George Abraham

In the image—any image—the Palestinian is dead. In the background, a field of rocks that once were homes, field of fallen flowers. Beyond the image, the Palestinian dies. And elsewhere, dies again. The Palestinian is witnessed dead. That witnessing, a kind of death. Of someone's child, of someone's sibling, of someone's *someone*. The ownership of the Palestinian body, and after-image of, as another kind of death. The circulation of the image as anti anti/ownership. Ours, in some disembodied landsense which, presuming we are living, can't be *ours*. The *ours* implicated as a kind of death. The anti/ownership constituted by our living as another death. The circulation of the image as a motion with a void at its center, beating. Void which says *look into me*, and festers in the un-looking. Void which is opposite of image, after of sounds's *after*. Not dis/embodied but the / between. The Palestinian dies in, and against, the image, any image. The Palestinian dies in the image, stone in hand. The Palestinian dies in the image, roof ablaze. The Palestinian dies in the landscape's impossible green. The Palestinian dies in, and as, rubble. In the image, a politics of verticality. Beneath settler's acid. Beneath settler's rain. Any image. The Palestinian dies on screen. The smartphone powered by dying acid. In the background of an image, a teenager, 3-lettered badge on their chest, machine gun pitched towards god, smiles into the sun, setting over the horizon of a Palestinian corpse. In the image, a reddening sea. The american, believing we are all fragments of fragments of the same dismembered starlight, rubs their face with our dead & oceanic, to perform an image they name *Birthright*. A european digs and. A country. The west shares the image. After which, there is no *after*. It is 2022. Westward, the

الكاميرا، عين الدولة. موتٌ يُطَهِّرُ الغربُ به موتَنا بتعاطفِهِم. سَهْلُ
الهَضْمِ حَتَّى الخَدَرِ. مَمْلُوكٌ، مَنْزُوعٌ مِنَ الخَيَالِ، في نِهَايَةِ المُطَافِ. الحَدُّ بَيْنَ
أَلِفٍ (أ) نَا وَأَلِفٍ (أ) رَشِيفٍ خَطٌّ مَرْسُومٌ بِالإِرْهَابِ. الفَرَاغُ في مَرْكَزِ
الصُّورَةِ المُتَدَاوَلَةِ، يُنَادِي عَلَيَّ بِكُلِّ أَسْمَائِي. أَنْ أَقِفَ عَلَى أُفُقِ الرُّعْبِ
ذَاتِهِ، وَأَقُول إِنَّ نَظَرِي، بِسَبَبِ حَيَاتِي، لَيْسَ كَافِيًا. أَنْ نُسَمِّيَهُ الهَدْمَ.
أَنْ نَتَجَاوَزَ بَيَاضَ الفَضَاءِ ذَاتِهِ، لِكَيْ نَبْحَثَ عَنْ عَوْدَةِ ذَوَاتِنَا وَسَطَ
فَوْضَى النُّجُومِ السَّاقِطَةِ. أَنْ أَسْتِي أَصْلِي المُتَشَابِكَ والمُضْطَرِبَ أمريكيًّا
مِن. أَنْ أَعْلَمَ أَنَّ مَا أَبْحَثُ عَنهُ سَيَتَطَلَّبُ مِن جَسَدِي، مِنَ العَدِيدِ مِنَ
الأجْسَادِ بَعدَهُ، عَدَدًا لَا يُمْكِنُ حصرهُ مِنَ المَيِّتَاتِ غَيرِ المَعْدُودَةِ

image is shared. The image, mistaken for an imperial siege on Ukraine, draws outrage beyond nation. *The image is a Palestinian image*, clarifies the Associated Press. The image dies again in dis-recognition. The *living* Palestinians die in the anti-mirror of the image's rot cycle. The Palestinians die in their living. The failure of these visual archives as a kind of death. Eye of camera, I of state. Death by which the west sanitizes our deaths with their empathy. Digestible until desensitized. Owned, dis-imagined, eventually. The border between *I* and *arch*(i)ve as a line drawn in terror. The void at the center of the image's circulation, calling my every name. To stand at the event horizon of terror itself, and say my gazing, because of my living, is not enough. To call it razing. To move beyond w(h)it(e)ness of space itself, so that we may search for the return of our selves amidst the chaos of fallen stars. To name my spiraling origin an america *of*. To know what I'm searching for will require, of my body, of the many selves beyond it, an unknowable number of uncountable deaths.

contributors

George Abraham (they/هو) is a Palestinian American poet, essayist, critic, and performance artist. Their debut poetry collection *Birthright* (Button Poetry, 2020) won the Arab American Book Award and was a Lambda Literary Award finalist. They are the executive editor of *Mizna*, and co-editor of *HEAVEN LOOKS LIKE US: Palestinian Poetry* (Haymarket Books, 2025). They are a graduate of Northwestern's Litowitz MFA+MA program, and teach at Amherst College as a Writer-in-Residence.

Eman Abukhadra is a Jordanian Canadian translator, interpreter, and poet of Palestinian origin. She holds a BA in Modern Languages and Literature and works between English, German, and Arabic. She translates poetry and other literary genres and has a particular interest in Palestinian, North African, and female voices.

Omar Aljaffal is an Iraqi journalist, researcher, and poet. His writings have appeared in a number of journals and magazines, and he has published two poetry collections. He was awarded the Mostafa Al-Hosseiny Prize for young Arab journalists in 2017.

Norah Alkharashi is a translator, scholar, and visual artist from Saudi Arabia and is currently completing a PhD in Translation Studies at the University of Ottawa. She has translated Edwidge Danticat's *The Dew Breaker* (*Kasir Al-Nada*, 2018) and *Everything Inside* (*Kul Shay' Bil-Dakhil*, 2024) into Arabic. Her English language translations, reviews and essays have been published in *ArabLit Quarterly, Banipal, Jadaliyya, Clina*, and in *River in an Ocean: Essays on Translation* (trace, 2023).

Lamia Abbas Amara (1929-2021) was born in Baghdad in a family of poets. She served on the board of the Union of Iraqi Writers from 1963 to 1975, and was Iraq's Deputy Permanent Representative to UNESCO in Paris from 1973 to 1975. She left Iraq in 1978 and lived most of her exile in San Diego, USA. Her most widely read poetry collections include *The Empty Corner*, *I Am Iraqi*, *Had the Fortune-teller Told Me*, and *Songs of Ishtar*.

Nour Balousha is a Palestinian poet, writer, and journalist based in Brussels. She is a member of the Palestine Writers Union, and contributes her expertise to numerous newspapers in the region. She is currently completing her MA thesis in Middle Eastern and North African Studies at Stockholm University.

Samar Diab is a Lebanese poet residing in Spain. She is the author of three poetry collections, *There is a Fight Outside* (2010), *Museum of Objects and Creatures* (2012), and *I Write Colourful Poems* (2021).

Najlaa Osman Eltom is a Sudanese poet, translator, academic, and activist currently based in Stockholm. She has published three volumes of poetry in Arabic. A collection of her poetry and prose, translated into English by Mayada Ibrahim, is forthcoming (trace press, 2026).

Miled Faiza is a Tunisian poet and translator. He is the author of *Baqāya l-bayt alladī dakalnāhu marratan wāḥida* (2004) and *Asabaʕ an-naḥḥāt* (2019). He has translated Ali Smith's Booker Prize shortlisted novel *Autumn* into Arabic (*al-Kharif*, 2017) as well as her novel *Winter* (*al-Shitā'*, 2019). He co-translated Shukri Mabkhout's *The Italian* into English (with Karen McNeil, Europa, 2021). He teaches Arabic at Brown University.

Zeena Faulk is an Iraqi American literary translator, interpreter, and literary scholar. She received her PhD in Translation Studies from the University of Warwick. Her literary translations have been published in *ArabLit Quarterly, Banipal* and other magazines. She is the Director of the Ettihad Cultural Center at Oregon State University.

Ibrahim Fawzy is a literary translator, writer, and editor from Egypt. He holds an MA in Comparative Literature, and has published translations, reviews, and interviews in numerous journals, including *ArabLit Quarterly, Words Without Borders, The Markaz Review, Modern Poetry in Translation, Poetry Birmingham Literary Journal*, and in *Best Literary Translations* (forthcoming, Deep Vellum, 2025). He received the 2023 PEN Presents award for his Arabic to English translation of Kuwaiti author Khalid Al Nasrallah's *The White Line of Night*.

Daad Haddad (1937-1991) was born in the coastal city of Lattakia and died in Damascus in 1991. She remained largely unrecognized in her lifetime within the male-dominated literary scene of Baathist Syria. She published two collections of poetry in the 1980s: *Correcting Death's Error* and *A Crust of Bread will Suffice Me*, with a third collection published shortly after her passing.

Yasmine Haj is a writer, editor, and translator from Nazareth, Palestine. She is the co-founder of Dalaala, a collective for the translation of art, cinema, and critical and literary texts. Her writings and translations have appeared in *Assafir, Assafir Al Arabi, Asymptote, Fikra Magazine, K-oh-llective, Romman Magazine, Specimen: The Babel Review of Translations, Best American Experimental Writing* (Wesleyan, 2020), and in *River in an Ocean: Essays on Translation* (trace, 2023).

Mayada Ibrahim is a literary translator, editor, and writer working between Arabic and English. She is based in Queens, New York, with roots in Khartoum and London. She is the co-recipient of the 2024 PEN Translates award, received the 2023 ALTA Travel Fellowship, and served as a judge for the 2021 PEN America Translation Award. Her translations have been published by Dolce Stil Criollo, 128 Lit, Foundry Editions, Archipelago, and Willows House in South Sudan. She is currently translating a collection of Najlaa Eltom's poetry and prose (forthcoming, trace 2026) and is the Managing Editor at Tilted Axis Press.

Rana Issa is a writer, translator, and cultural producer focusing on literary and contemporary artistic practices entangled with Arabic cultural history. She works at the intersection between public humanities, activist engagements, and academic curiosity. She is a co-founder and artistic director of Masahat. no, a dissemination platform for Arab art and culture in exile. Her work has appeared in leading journals, platforms, and presses, and she collaborates with international artists in the fields of film, performance arts, visual arts and sculpture. She is the author of *The Modern Arabic Bible* (Edinburgh University Press, 2023).

Ali Mahmoud Khudayyir is an Iraqi poet, writer, journalist, editor, and literary critic from Basra. He has published nine books of prose and poetry, and his poems have been translated into English, French, and Persian. He received the UNESCO International Literary Prize for Poetry in 2013, and the Young Poet Award from the Baghdad organization Culture for All. He is the founder of the Poetry Club in Basra and serves on the editorial board of the journal *Aqlam*.

Karen McNeil is a scholar and translator. She co-translated Shukri Mabkhout's *The Italian* (with Miled Faiza), and has translated poems and short stories for *Banipal* and *World Literature Today*. She was a revising editor of the *Oxford Arabic Dictionary* (2014) and is currently completing a PhD in Arabic linguistics at Georgetown University, with a focus on the sociolinguistics of Tunisia.

Hiba Moustafa is an emerging literary translator and poet with an interest in feminist literature. She has translated poems and essays by Lucille Clifton, Angela Davis, bell hooks, and Mona Eltahawy into Arabic for *Rusted Radishes, Hikayat Baladi, Aperture, Elles*, and Saqi Books. Her English translations of Arabic poetry have appeared in *ArabLit Quarterly*. She holds an MA in English Literature and currently translates for *My Kali* magazine.

Suneela Mubayi is a translator, writer, and independent scholar with a PhD in Arabic literature from NYU. She is interested in gender and sexual liberation, and the intersections of language, the body, and poetry. She has taught Arabic language and literature in the US and the UK and translated over a hundred essays, poems, and fiction pieces between Arabic, English, and Urdu for various publications including *Banipal, Words Without Borders, Asymptote, Jadaliyya, Mada Masr*, and others. Her critical and creative essays have appeared in various journals, and in *River in an Ocean: Essays on Translation* (trace, 2023).

Mariam Naji is an Egypt-based literary translator and writer. She holds a degree in English Literature from Assiut University and has translated Stephanie Land's *Maid* and Lucey Foley's *The Guest List* into English (Aseer Al Kotob, 2023). Her writings and translations have appeared in in *Manshoor, Al-Hudood, Al Jazeera*, and *Mada Masr*, Boring Books, and TakweenKW. She has received the 2021 Arabic Translation Mentorship from New Writing North and the British Council for Emerging Translators.

Ibrahim Nasrallah is a Palestinian poet, novelist, professor, painter, and photographer. He was born in a Palestinian refugee camp in Jordan to parents evicted from their land in Al-Burayj, Palestine in 1948. He has written fifteen poetry collections and twenty-two novels and received several prizes for his work, including the International Prize for Arabic Fiction and the Katara Prize. His writing has been translated into English, Spanish, Danish, Turkish, and Persian.

Kamal Nasser (1924-1973) was born in Gaza, and grew up in Bir Zeit near Ramallah. He graduated from the American University of Beirut and initially worked as an Arabic teacher, and later as a lawyer, before dedicating himself to a life of journalism and political activism. He was elected into the PLO Executive Committee and headed its information office until he became the PLO spokesperson in 1969. Nasser was martyred on April 10th, 1973, on Verdun Street in Beirut, in a Mossad operation led by Ehud Barak who became Israel's Prime Minister in 1999.

Nashwa Nasreldin is a poet, writer, editor, and translator of Arabic literature. She has translated *Shatila Stories*, a collaborative novel by nine refugee writers (Peirene, 2018), and co-translated Samar Yazbek's memoir, *The Crossing: My Journey to the Shattered Heart of Syria* (Rider, 2015). Nashwa holds an MFA in Writing from the Vermont College of Fine Arts. Her poetry, translations, articles, and reviews have been published in the UK and internationally. She has worked with *ArabLit Quarterly* and is Editor at the Poetry Translation Centre, UK.

Nofel is a Montréal based poet and essayist, writing in English and Arabic. His writing has been published by the *League of Canadian Poets*, and has appeared in *Geist, Canadian Notes & Queries, Contemporary Verse 2, Plenitude Magazine* and *The Ex-Puritan*. Nofel was longlisted for the CBC 2022 Nonfiction Prize, and two of his poems are featured in *El Ghourabaa: A Queer and Trans Collection of Oddities* (Metonymy, 2024).

Lena Khalaf Tuffaha is a poet, essayist, translator, and literary curator. She is the author of three books of poetry: *Something About Living* (University of Akron), finalist for the 2024 National Book Award and winner of the 2022 Akron Prize for Poetry; *Kaan & Her Sisters* (Trio House), finalist for the 2024 Firecracker Award and honorable mention for the 2024 Arab American Book Award, and *Water & Salt* (Red Hen), winner of the 2018 Washington State Book Award and honorable mention for 2018 Arab American Award. She is the author of two chapbooks, *Arab in Newsland*, winner of the 2016 Two Sylvias Prize, and *Letters from the Interior* (Diode, 2019) finalist for the 2020 Jean Pedrick Chapbook Prize.

Fadwa Tuqan (1917-2003) is a renowned Palestinian poet whose award-winning writings have been translated into several languages. Her publications include eight collections of poetry and two memoirs. Born to a politically influential family, Tuqan's poetry voiced her resistance to the Israeli occupation and her defiance of social customs. She died in December 2003, at the height of the second Palestinian intifada, when her ancestral hometown of Nablus was under siege.

Qasim Saudi is an Iraqi poet and writer. He is the founder of the Let's Write project in Baghdad, and leader of the Writing Marathon initiative that teaches primary school students to write children's short stories. His poetry collection, *The Musician's Chair*, won Oman's Atheer Poetry Prize in 2014. He is also an accomplished children's story writer with numerous publications.

credits

Abraham, George. "Field Notes on Terror & Beginnings."*Poetry Daily*, July 6, 2023.

ابراهام، جورج. "ملاحظات ميدانية حول الإرهاب والبدايات." مجلة الشعر اليومية، ٦ يوليو ٢٠٢٣.

Amara, Lamia Abbas. *Law Anba'ani Al-'Arraf* [If the Fortune Teller Told Me]. Beirut: Al-Mu'assasa Al-'Arabiyya lil-Dirasat wa-l-Nashr, 1985.

عمارة، لميعة عباس. لو أنبأني العرّاف. بيروت: المؤسسة العربية للدراسات والنشر، ١٩٨٥.

Ba'lusha, Noor. "Atfi'oo Hathihi al-Nar." *Majallat Fus'ha - Thaqafiyya Filastiniyya*, January 13, 2024.

بعلوشة، نور. "أطفئوا هذه الحرب." مجلة فُسْحَة - ثقافيّة فلسطينيّة، ١٣ يناير ٢٠٢٤.

Diab, Samar. *Mat'haf al-Ashya' wa al-Ka'inat* [Museum of Objects and Things]. Beirut: Dar Al-Ghawoon, 2013.

دياب، سمر. متحف الأشياء والكائنات. بيروت: دار الغاوون، ٢٠١٣.

Diab, Samar. *Aktub Qasa'id Mulawwana* [I Write Colored Poems]. Damascus: Dar Kan'an Publishing House, 2021.

دياب، سمر. أكتب قصائد ملونة. دمشق. دار كنعان. ٢٠٢١.

Eltom, Najlaa. *Al-Jarimah al-Khalidah That al-Aqraṭ* [The Eternal Crime with The Earrings]. Juba: Rafiki Publishing House, 2019.

التوم، نجلاء. الجريمة الخالدة ذات الأقراط. جوبا: دار رفقي للنشر، ٢٠١٩.

Haddad, Da'd. *Ana Allati Tabki min Shiddat Al-She'r* [I Am the One Who Cries from the Intensity of Poetry]. Damascus: Dar Al-Takween Publishing House, 2018.

حداد، دعد. أنا التي تبكي من شدة الشعر. دمشق: دار التكوين، ٢٠١٨.

Mahmoud, Ali. *Salyl al-Ghaymah* [The Shadow of the Cloud]. Basrah: Manshurat Basora, 2015.

محمود، علي. سليل الغيمة. البصرة: منشورات باصورا، ٢٠١٥.

Miled, Faiza. *'Asabi' al-Naḥḥat* [The Sculptor's Fingers]. Algiers: Dar Mayara, 2019.

ميلاد، فايزة. أصابع النحات. الجزائر: دار ميارة، ٢٠١٩.

Nasser, Kamal. *Al-Daw' Al-Akhdar: Al-Athar Al-She'riya* [The Green Light: The Poetic Works]. Beirut: Al-Mu'assasa Al-Arabiya lil-Dirasat wal-Nashr, 1974.

ناصر،كمال. الضّوء الأخضر: الآثار الشعرية. بيروت: المؤسسة العربية للدراسات والنشر، ١٩٧٤.

Nasrallah, Ibrahim. *Hatab Akhdar* [Green Wood]. Amman: Dar Al Shorouq lil-Nashr wal-Tawzee', 1991.

نصر الله، إبراهيم. حطب أخضر. عمان: دار الشروق للنشر والتوزيع، ١٩٩١.

Saudi, Qasim. *Mithl Qarib Khashabi Maqlub fi al-Sahra* [Like an Upside-Down Wooden Boat in the Desert]. Baghdad: Ma'na Translation and Publishing, 2017.

سعودي، قاسم. مثل قارب خشبي مقلوب في الصحراء. بغداد: معنى للترجمة والنشر، ٢٠١٧.

Tuqan, Fadwa. *Qira'at al-Mahthoof: Qasa'ed Lam Tunshiruha Fadwa Tuqan* [Readings of the Omitted: Poems Unpublished by Fadwa Tuqan]. Amman: Dar Al Shorouq lil-Nashr wal-Tawzee', 2004.

طوقان، فدوى. قراءة المحذوف: قصائد لم تنشرها فدوى طوقان. عمان: دار الشروق للنشر والتوزيع. ٢٠٠٤.

Tuffaha, Lena Khalaf. *Water & Salt*. California: Red Hen Press, 2017.

تفاحة، لينا خلف. ماء وملح. كاليفورنيا: دار ريد هن للنشر، ٢٠١٧.

t r a c e is both verb and noun; act and residue.

t r a c e collaborates with writers to publish books that illuminate, in complex, beautiful, and thought-provoking ways, contemporary and historical experiences of conflict, war, displacement, exile, migration, the environment, labour, and resistance.

We look for words that draw connections between here and there; now and then. Voices that ask us to question, reflect, take pleasure, love, remember, and build solidarity across our many differences.

We are unafraid to mix genres, voices, and languages.

t r a c e is a not-for-profit press.

We invite you to support our work.

tracepress.org